DATE DUE

| APR 0 2 2009 | |
| --- | --- |
| | |
| MAY 1 7 2012 | |
| | |
| | |
| | |
| | |
| | |
| | |
| | |
| | |
| | |
| | |
| | |

# MARCHING TO
# APPOMATTOX
## The Footrace That Ended the Civil War

★ *Ken Stark* ★

**G. P. PUTNAM'S SONS**

"... let us strive on to finish the work we are in; to bind up the nation's wounds; to care for him who shall have borne the battle, and for his widow, and his orphan—to do all which may achieve and cherish a just, and a lasting peace, among ourselves, and with all nations."

PRESIDENT ABRAHAM LINCOLN'S
SECOND INAUGURAL ADDRESS,
MARCH 4, 1865

# FOREWORD

**Abraham Lincoln**

**Jefferson Davis**

Americans were uneasy on Inauguration Day, March 4, 1861. President-elect Abraham Lincoln appealed to the South: "In *your* hands, my dissatisfied fellow countrymen, and not in *mine*, is the momentous issue of civil war. . . . We must not be enemies."

It was no use. Bitter Southern states believed Lincoln planned to tear down slavery and with it their way of life. One by one, they were breaking from the United States to form the Confederate States of America. The new country's president was fiery Jefferson Davis.

"No human power," he said, "can save the Union." Lincoln took a solemn oath to do exactly that. The cost was high.

On April 12, Confederate cannons blasted U.S. Fort Sumter in Charleston Harbor, South Carolina. War was on! The North would fight to keep all of the states in the Union—the South, for independence. Each side expected victory in just months.

Almost four years later, more than 600,000 American soldiers were dead. War raged on, and the Confederacy was fast losing ground and soldiers. But it still had General Robert E. Lee, the idol of his men. He and his hungry Army of Northern Virginia hung on—the South's last hope!

# THE RACE: LEE AGAINST GRANT
## APRIL 3–9, 1865

CONFEDERATE TROOPS    UNION TROOPS    MAJOR BATTLES

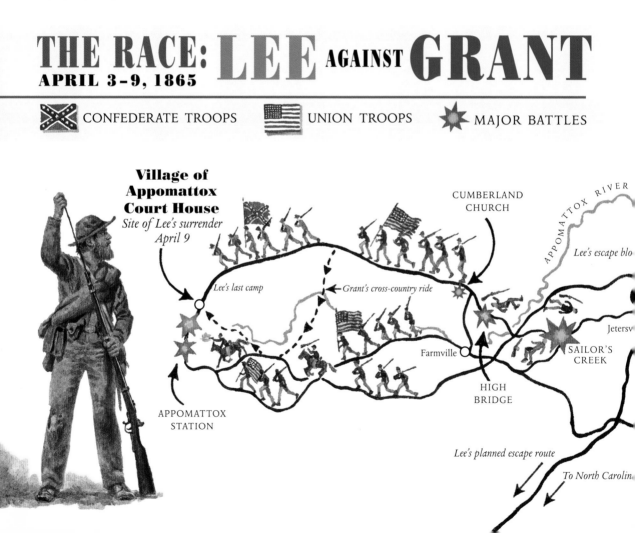

**Village of Appomattox Court House**
*Site of Lee's surrender April 9*

CUMBERLAND CHURCH

APPOMATTOX RIVER

Lee's escape blo

Lee's last camp

Grant's cross-country ride

Jetersv

Farmville

SAILOR'S CREEK

APPOMATTOX STATION

HIGH BRIDGE

Lee's planned escape route

To North Carolina

The North had iron-willed Lieutenant General Ulysses S. Grant. On April 2, 1865, he ordered an all-out attack to end his nine-month siege of Petersburg, Virginia. Grant hoped it would be the last battle. War-saddened Lincoln prayed he was right.

Grant's Army of the Potomac overwhelmed the Confederate stronghold. Lee was forced to retreat in the night, abandoning Petersburg and nearby Richmond, the Confederate capital and heart of the rebellion. The next morning, freed slaves celebrated as Union troops marched into Richmond. Fireworks burst in the North and tears fell in the South. Down came the Rebel flag. Up flew the Stars and Stripes.

"Thank God that I have lived to see this!" said Lincoln.

But Lincoln's joy meant misery for fleeing President Davis. His country was crumbling, yet he declared, "I will not consent to abandon one foot [of Confederate soil.]" He ordered Lee to fight to the end.

To save the Confederacy, and themselves, General Lee and his somber soldiers in gray needed a miracle. They were marching away to find it.

Chasing them were General Grant and his U.S. Armies in blue. This was the footrace that would end the war.

**Robert E. Lee**

**Ulysses S. Grant**

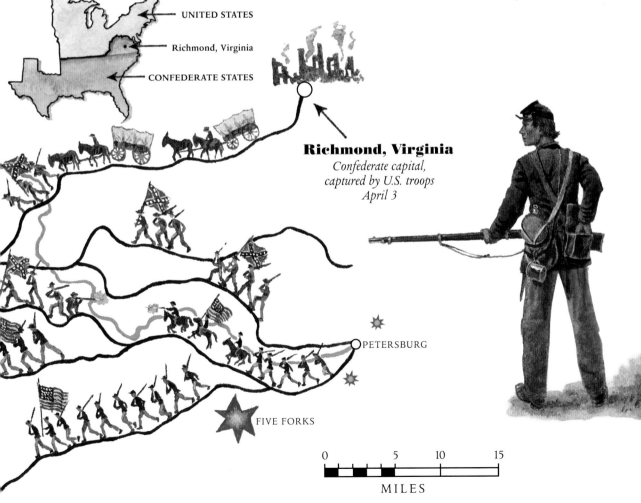

UNITED STATES

Richmond, Virginia

CONFEDERATE STATES

**Richmond, Virginia**
*Confederate capital, captured by U.S. troops April 3*

PETERSBURG

FIVE FORKS

0   5   10   15

MILES

# ★ APRIL 3, 1865, SOUTHERN VIRGINIA

*We are after Lee, and we are going to have him.*
UNION LIEUTENANT COLONEL ELISHA HUNT RHODES

It was the fourth spring of the Civil War. Northern soldiers pounded through Virginia, itching to stop the Southern rebellion that divided America. Muddy water squirted from their shoes. Sweat ran down their sunburned faces. Everywhere the Bluecoats went, warnings sped ahead of them: "The Yankees are coming! The whole world is coming!"

**E**ighty thousand United States soldiers were chasing the Confederate Army of Northern Virginia, the South's strongest army. Union officers shouted, "Your legs must do it, boys!" White troops and black troops—all in blue—stepped quicker. They laughed and sang. If the Yanks caught the Rebel army, the war would end and so would slavery.

One Bluecoat, a plainspoken store clerk from Illinois, had determination carved in his face. He was forty-two-year-old Ulysses S. Grant. Gone was his boyhood nickname, "Useless." Now he was lieutenant general, Abraham Lincoln's top officer. The whole North depended on him. Night and day, he rode Cincinnati, the tall son of a racehorse, or his smaller mount, Jeff Davis. Grant hardly had a minute to think of his wife and four children. In all the hurry-scurry, some generals bellowed and cursed. Not steady Grant. He only got angry when he saw a man hurt a horse. And he talked so little, officers joked that he could be "silent in several languages."

All business, Grant slouched in his wrinkled, dirty uniform. He constantly puffed cigars and studied maps. Could he do as the President wished—capture General Robert E. Lee's army without another bloody battle? Grant calmly gave the orders: "Get ahead of him and cut him off." Lee must not escape to drag out the war.

General Lee's outnumbered Confederates tramped ahead, some fifty thousand men and boys in shabby gray or butternut. Somehow, the gray-bearded Lee had to shake off Grant and hurry down to North Carolina. Joe Johnston's army was there. Together they might hold out until the North tired of war, and the South got what it wanted—independence.

Lee tried to be hopeful. He had a day's head start on the enemy— "those people," he called them. But cannons sank in the mud and bridges washed out. If only his rail-thin troops could stay in front. He knew Grant would not let up for a minute. Whatever might happen, Lee was a loyal Virginian, determined to do his duty and fight on.

His spread-out army struggled west on four roads. Lee splashed down one of them on his favorite horse, Traveller. People strained to see the famous top commander. A woman along the way wrote, "Everyone was under the spell of his presence and dignity." At fifty-eight, the handsome leader still fit his old nickname, "The Marble Model." He didn't drink, smoke or swear. Lee's only habit was outsmarting the Yanks. His men loved him for it.

But how his fighters hated retreating from the "Yankee invaders" they used to beat like clockwork. Their hearts ached and their bellies growled. They chewed hard corn that only horses liked. Worn-down men dropped, limp as old socks. Others, sick of fighting, stole away for home. Most marched on, scarecrows with guns. On for the South and for Robert E. Lee!

*The road is filled with broken wagons and the things thrown away in the flight of the Rebels.*
UNION LIEUTENANT COLONEL ELISHA HUNT RHODES

Lee buttoned every button and rode ramrod-straight. Kindly and cheerfully, he encouraged his men. They hollered, "Hurrah, Uncle Robert! Hurrah!"

But Lee's strong face drained when they reached Amelia Court House. Expected rations weren't there—not one cracker for his hungry army. Lee had to halt his troops and send detachments to comb the countryside for food. They found little, searching all night. Lee tried to hide his despair. His army was stalled, and its precious lead melted away. On top of that, mounted Yankees were making hit-and-run raids. Meanwhile, other Yanks pushed hard on a separate road, trying to get ahead of the Rebels.

# ★ APRIL 5, JETERSVILLE

*Tired and hungry we push on. It is now a race for life or death.*

CONFEDERATE LIEUTENANT COLONEL WILLIAM M. OWEN

Lee's troubles were piling higher and higher. This drizzly day, he prodded his soggy troops south to escape. At Jetersville, though, he ran into a solid wall of blue. Those hotfooted Yanks had beaten them there and were now dug in thick and deep. This was another stomach blow to Lee. His careful plans were ruined. How could he feed his weakening soldiers and dodge Grant, much less get to North Carolina? Frustrated, Lee turned his army west again, the only way open. Miles of half-dreaming Graycoats stumbled through the night. Marching boys with muskets fell asleep on their feet. They smacked the ground and woke up fast.

Under the same dim moon, every Billy Yank stomped after
Lee like he was a lottery prize. Grant was confident in his
quiet, unsmiling way. Near midnight, he nudged Cincinnati
on a perilous ride through enemy country to meet with his
generals, hard-fighting Philip Sheridan and crusty George
Meade.

Grant put it simply: "Lee's surely in a bad fix. It will be
difficult for him to get away." Still, Grant knew if there was a
way out, Lee would find it.

# ★ APRIL 6, SAILOR'S CREEK

*This will be the last battle if we win, and then you and I can go home.*
UNION CAPTAIN CHARLES W. GLEASON, KILLED AT SAILOR'S CREEK

While Lee rode miles ahead with the front of his Army, hard-marching Bluecoats cut off its slow-moving tail at Sailor's Creek. Cannons thundered. Bullets peppered the air. Shouts! Screams! Boys with peach fuzz fell. Fathers and grandfathers fell. Hundreds on both sides would never go home. Nearly eight thousand gloomy Rebels—including Lee's son Custis—held their guns high in surrender. That suited Grant. He wanted prisoners, not their graves.

Coming on the scene, Lee was grim. One fifth of his army was captured. "My God!" he groaned. "Has the army been dissolved?"

Suddenly, Lee grabbed a Confederate battle flag and held it up to rally his remaining men. They flocked to the gray general, inspired by his resolve.

*This Army is hopelessly whipped . . . the blood of every man who
is killed from this time forth is on your head, General Lee.*

CONFEDERATE GENERAL HENRY WISE

**L**ee kept on, his half-starved men fighting for every mile. Lee told his other son, a general named Rooney: "Keep your command together and in good spirits . . . I will get you out of this."

Grant, though, knew the once-mighty Rebel army was finished. If only he could convince Lee.

Mud-splattered to his whiskers, his face tense, Grant swung off Cincinnati and took a step toward peace. On a hotel porch, he wrote Lee a polite, but formal note:

> *General: The results of the last week must convince you of the hopelessness of further resistance on the part of the Army of Northern Virginia in this struggle. I feel that it is so, and regard it as my duty to shift from myself the responsibility of any further effusion of blood, by asking of you the surrender of that portion of the [Confederate States] Army known as the Army of Northern Virginia.*
>
> > *Very respectfully,*
> > *Your obedient servant,*
> > *U. S. Grant,*
> > *Lieutenant General,*
> > *Commanding Armies of the U. S.*

A messenger started his dangerous ride to enemy lines. Grant waited into the night. He watched his worn-out armies of the Potomac and of the James trudging after Lee. He was proud of them. Their heavy legs stepped lively. "Grant! Grant!" chanted the men. They lit torches and sang the anti-slavery anthem "John Brown's Body." Victory was near. They could feel it.

At a late hour, Lee and Lieutenant General James "Pete" Longstreet, his second in command, pondered the letter. There would be no surrender. "Not yet," said Longstreet, and Lee agreed. He still believed his duty was to fight for the South, though its cause seemed lost. Southerners were counting on him. Bone-tired, Lee wrote Grant by candlelight:

> *General: I have received your note of this day. Though not entertaining the opinion you express on the hopelessness of further resistance on the part of the Army of Northern Virginia, I reciprocate your desire to avoid useless effusion of blood, and therefore, before considering your proposition, ask the terms you will offer on condition of its surrender.*
>
> *Very respectfully, your obedient servant,*
> *R. E. Lee, General*

Early in the frosty morning, Grant wrote back:

> *. . . peace being my great desire, there is but one condition . . . that the men and officers surrendered shall be disqualified for taking up arms again against the Government of the United States . . .*

# ★ APRIL 8, THE ROADS TO APPOMATTOX COURT HOUSE

*We knew by our own aching hearts that his [Lee's] was breaking.*

CONFEDERATE MAJOR GENERAL JOHN B. GORDON

The war did not wait for the pens. Each side sweated and strained to out-step the other. Half the Yanks chased the Rebels, and half marched pell-mell on other routes to get in front. All were hungry as wolves.

Rations waited for Lee's men at Appomattox Station, a railroad hamlet ahead. The Graycoats desperately needed the food. The Blues were determined to keep them from it.

Some Confederates too weak to carry their muskets threw them away or stabbed them in the ground. Exhausted horses and mules collapsed and rolled their eyes. Idle wagons were burned. Useless cannons were buried to keep them out of enemy hands. Some of Lee's own officers knew it was time to quit. But Lee said firmly, "I trust it has not come to that. Indeed, we must all determine to die at our posts."

Now one hundred miles into the race, the weary enemies were almost neck and neck. They stomped west on different roads that met ahead at Appomattox Court House, a peaceful village in the path of war. No one in Appomattox would sleep well this night.

Union horsemen led by Major General George Custer thundered upon surprised Confederates at the nearby railroad station. Fireflies blinked and cannons dueled. In a furious battle, the Yanks seized trainloads of vital rations, then rushed to box Lee in at last.

In his woodland camp outside Appomattox, Lee fought back emotions. Should he give in or fight? He conferred with his generals and made up his mind—break free at dawn. Then Lee bedded down, not knowing if his army would live another day.

Some miles behind Lee, General Grant could hardly think. A blinding headache had struck him in the afternoon. The pain kept him up. Around midnight, a message came from Lee:

> *I do not think the emergency has arisen to call for the surrender of this army . . .*

Grant held his head and muttered, "I believe he means to fight."

## ★ APRIL 9, APPOMATTOX COURT HOUSE

*If the Army of Northern Virginia surrenders, every other army will surrender...*

CONFEDERATE BRIGADIER GENERAL EDWARD PORTER ALEXANDER

Grant wrote Lee one last time, asking him to give in. It was too late. Rebel cannons cracked the foggy dawn at Appomattox. Bayonets bristled like porcupine quills. Lee's gaunt fighters swatted away the small Union cavalry that had blocked his route west. Escape seemed possible. Goose bumps rose with the chilling Rebel yell, a screeching "whooo-whoo."

It died when thousands of Union troops—white and black—came into view. They had marched thirty-six miles in twenty-four hours to slam the last door on the Confederates. The long race was over. The proud Army of Northern Virginia was trapped.

Lee sent an order, and a horseman galloped from the tattered gray ranks. He flew a white towel, a makeshift flag of truce. Yanks and Rebels froze. Eyes gazed, unbelieving.

**W**as this truly the end?

General Lee knew it was. Some of his rugged men covered their faces and cried. Others broke their guns on trees. They hated giving up. One general urged Lee to scatter the army so it could fight on, guerilla-style. But Lee knew that would mean more misery, more widows, more fatherless children. Lee said no.

His voice was thick. "There is nothing left me to do now but to go and see General Grant, and I would rather die a thousand deaths." Expecting to be Grant's prisoner, Lee wore his best uniform with sash and sword. He sat forlorn, under an apple tree, while his last message headed for Grant.

Back on the battlefield, some Union generals wanted to smash the Rebels. They thought the white flag was a trick, but they decided to hold back for two hours. Only Grant could make the truce official, and he wasn't there yet.

Far away, Grant and his staff skirted Rebels who had a chance to make Grant himself a prisoner. He had been behind Lee to stay in quicker communication with him. Now Grant rode rapidly cross-country toward Appomattox. With every hoofbeat, his head pounded harder.

Around noon, time was running out. Grant was still miles from the village when an officer galloped up, shouting and waving his hat. He had Lee's message. Grant read it and grew pale. Lee would surrender! Instantly, his two-day headache was gone. The note was then read aloud to his staff. There was silence, followed by tears of joy. Four years of killing were over!

Grant hurriedly dictated one last note to Lee: "I . . . will push forward to the front for the purpose of meeting you." Grant rode on, perhaps with a rare smile.

The commanders needed a suitable place to meet in Appomattox. A merchant named Wilmer McLean offered his fine brick house. The parlor would do. McLean's daughter Lula had been playing there, but dropped her rag doll on the horsehair sofa and was shooed from the room.

Lee was first to arrive, somber yet magnificent on his famous Traveller.

Soon, house slaves in back saw their freedom ride up on a chestnut horse. It was U. S. Grant, rumpled and dirty after his long ride on Cincinnati. The two warhorses grazed peacefully.

Inside, the rivals Lee and Grant shook hands. Lula's doll sat unnoticed. Officers later called her "the silent witness."

Lee was tall, erect and splendidly dressed. Was he glad it was all over or heartsick at defeat? Dignity masked his feelings. Grant worried that his plain, dingy uniform insulted the Southern gentleman. Even more, he felt sad at the fall of his adversary who had fought so long and bravely for his beliefs.

Each respected the other, but not his cause.

Soon spurs jangled, and the parlor was filled with hushed Union officers. The two head generals made small talk like neighbors. Then, thoughtfully, in his own words, Grant penciled the surrender terms. They were as kind and generous as President Lincoln had wanted. No one would be punished. The Rebels needed only to stack their arms and go home in peace. Grant promised to let Lee's men who owned a horse or mule take the animal to work their farms. Lee's face softened.

He said, "This will have the best possible effect on the men."

The time came to copy the documents in ink. A nervous Union officer botched two attempts. Lieutenant Colonel Ely Parker took over. He was Grant's friend and aide. He was also a Seneca Indian Chief. Parker checked for errors, then copied the words that closed the catastrophic war.

Lee and Grant signed their names, and it was done.

Outside, the two leaders tipped their hats and parted. Lee smoothed Traveller's forelock and rode slowly through his crowding men. Their eyes swam at the sight of Lee's downcast face. They touched Traveller and kissed him. They felt Lee's gloves and boots. A man called, "I love you as well as ever, General Lee." Again and again his steadfast men cried out, "Good-bye, General. God bless you."

"I have done my best for you," Lee said. "My heart is too full to say more."

General Grant was not one for speeches. He rode swiftly away to his headquarters tent.

The word was out: "We are going home!" Men in blue jumped like gymnasts. Everywhere, they laughed and cried for joy.

A young soldier noted: "The men threw their knapsacks and canteens into the air and howled like mad." Some fired guns and cannons to celebrate. Grant made them stop. The Southerners had suffered enough, he thought.

Grant told his men, "The war is over. The Rebels are our countrymen again."

Now, the Blues and the Grays did not trade gunfire. They swapped pocketknives and knickknacks as souvenirs. Yankees shared their few rations with Rebels. They had a smoke, a cup of coffee.

Ahead was a long walk home to their families and to one country.
"So long, Yank."
"Good-bye, Johnny Reb."

The heart went out of the South's long fight for independence when Lee surrendered his 28,000 beleaguered men to Grant at Appomattox on April 9, 1865. Essentially, the war was over. Scattered shooting ended for good a few weeks later in the far South and West.

The long, complicated work of Reconstruction began. The Union would be restored, and slavery was dead, but bitterness festered like a wound.

President Lincoln's plans to heal the nation were shattered on April 14. A Southern sympathizer named John Wilkes Booth snuck up behind him at a lighthearted play and fired a pistol. Mortally wounded, Abraham Lincoln died the next morning. Millions grieved.

While Lincoln's funeral train rolled across the country, a Union soldier fatally shot Booth in a Virginia barn on April 26. That same day, General Joseph E. Johnston, leader of the last large Confederate army, surrendered in North Carolina. Jefferson Davis hoped to fight on, but he was captured in Georgia on May 10 and imprisoned for two years. The last Confederate force surrendered on June 2.

Robert E. Lee lost his citizenship for his role in the rebellion and was never pardoned. Still, he urged people to forget grudges against the North and to obey the United States government. Widely respected, Lee became president of Washington College in Lexington, Virginia. He and Traveller enjoyed long rides together until sixty-three-year-old Lee became ill and died in 1870. The famous warhorse died the next year.

Ulysses S. Grant was elected U.S. president in 1868, thanks in part to black voters. He served two terms. Grant favored equal rights for blacks and tried to stamp out the rising Ku Klux Klan. Late in life, he fought throat cancer while writing his memoirs to support his family. He showed the same determination in this as on the roads to Appomattox, and lived just long enough to finish. Grant died in 1885, at age sixty-three.

The Civil War remains the deadliest in America's history. Roughly 204,000 soldiers and sailors were killed in battle, and 420,000 died from diseases or other causes.

# SELECTED BIBLIOGRAPHY

Calkins, Chris M. *The Battles of Appomattox Station and Appomattox Court House, April 8–9, 1865.* Lynchburg, Virginia: H. E. Howard, Inc.: second edition, 1987.

Catton, Bruce. *A Stillness at Appomattox.* Garden City, New York: Doubleday and Company, 1953.

Davis, Burke. *To Appomattox: Nine April Days, 1865.* New York: Holt, Rinehart and Winston, 1959.

Foote, Shelby. *The Civil War, A Narrative: Red River to Appomattox.* New York: Random House, Volume 3 [1958–1974].

Grant, Ulysses S. *Personal Memoirs of Ulysses S. Grant.* New York: Charles L. Webster Company, 1886. Volume 2.

National Park Service. *Appomattox Court House: Appomattox Court House National Historical Park, Virginia.* Division of Publications, Harpers Ferry Center, N. P. S., 2002.

Rhodes, Robert Hunt (editor). *All for the Union—1865, The Civil War Diary and Letters of Elisha Hunt Rhodes.* Lincoln, Rhode Island: A. Mowbray, 1985.

Smith, Gene. *Lee and Grant, A Dual Biography.* New York: McGraw-Hill, 1984.

Smith, Robin, and Ron Field. *Uniforms of the Civil War: An Illustrated Guide for Historians, Collectors, and Reenactors.* Guilford, Connecticut: Lyons Press, 2001.

Trudeau, Noah Andre. *The Campaign to Appomattox, National Parks Civil War Series.* Conshohocken, Pennsylvania: Eastern National Park and Monument Association, 1995.

Ward, Geoffrey C., with Ric Burns and Ken Burns. *The Civil War: An Illustrated History.* New York: Alfred A. Knopf, Inc., 1990.

★ *To my nephews Bill, Ken, and Greg* ★

ACKNOWLEDGMENTS

Special thanks to my wife, Chris, for her research assistance and endless support. I am also grateful to the staff at Appomattox Court House National Historical Park, Appomattox, Virginia, especially historian Patrick A. Schroeder for his critical review of the text and art. Thank you to Lynette Owens, director of the Viola Public Library, Viola, Wisconsin; the library and museum staff of the Wisconsin Historical Society; Marilyn Onorati, librarian of the Amelia Historical Society, Amelia, Virginia; and to Vaughn Stanley, James Leyburn Library special collections librarian at Washington and Lee University, Lexington, Virginia.

G. P. PUTNAM'S SONS
A division of Penguin Young Readers Group.
Published by The Penguin Group.
Penguin Group (USA) Inc., 375 Hudson Street, New York, NY 10014, U.S.A. Penguin Group (Canada), 90 Eglinton Avenue East, Suite 700, Toronto, Ontario M4P 2Y3, Canada (a division of Pearson Penguin Canada Inc.). Penguin Books Ltd, 80 Strand, London WC2R 0RL, England. Penguin Ireland, 25 St. Stephen's Green, Dublin 2, Ireland (a division of Penguin Books Ltd.). Penguin Group (Australia), 250 Camberwell Road, Camberwell, Victoria 3124, Australia (a division of Pearson Australia Group Pty Ltd). Penguin Books India Pvt Ltd, 11 Community Centre, Panchsheel Park, New Delhi—110 017, India. Penguin Group (NZ), 67 Apollo Drive, Rosedale, North Shore 0632, New Zealand (a division of Pearson New Zealand Ltd). Penguin Books (South Africa) (Pty) Ltd, 24 Sturdee Avenue, Rosebank, Johannesburg 2196, South Africa. Penguin Books Ltd, Registered Offices: 80 Strand, London WC2R 0RL, England.

Manufactured in China by South China Printing Co. Ltd.
Design by Richard Amari.
Text set in Columbus.
The art was done in watercolor, gouache, and casein.

Library of Congress Cataloging-in-Publication Data
Stark, Ken. Marching to Appomattox : the footrace that ended the Civil War / Ken Stark. p. cm. Includes bibliographical references. 1. Appomattox Campaign, 1865—Juvenile literature. 2. Lee, Robert E. (Robert Edward), 1807–1870—Juvenile literature. 3. Grant, Ulysses S. (Ulysses Simpson), 1822–1885—Juvenile literature. 4. United States—History—Civil War, 1861–1865—Peace—Juvenile literature. I. Title.
E477.67.S73 2009    973.7'38—dc22    2008012551
ISBN 978-0-399-24212-0
1 3 5 7 9 10 8 6 4 2